Delicious breakfasts

Delicious breakfasts

Cover and internal design by Mark Cavanagh
Introduction by Bridget Jones
Photography by Don Last
Additional photography by Gunter Beer
Home Economist Christine Last

ISBN 978-1-4075-0120-8
Printed in China

Notes for the reader
• This book uses imperial, metric and US cup measurements. Follow the same units of measurement throughout; do not mix imperial and metric.
• All spoon measurements are level: teaspoons are assumed to be 5 ml and tablespoons are assumed to be 15 ml.
• Unless otherwise stated, milk is assumed to be whole and eggs are medium. The times given are an approximate guide only.
• Some recipes contain nuts. If you are allergic to nuts you should avoid using them and any products containing nuts. Recipes using raw or very lightly cooked eggs should be avoided by infants, the elderly, pregnant women, convalescents, and anyone suffering from illness.

Contents

Breakfasts

Early bird or night owl, no matter when you feel energetic, breakfast is important for vitality. It will awaken your mind, re-balance your body, and provide energy and rejuvenating nutrients to keep you ahead of the morning and on track all day.

By morning, the body has digested yesterday's meals. Many people feel grumpy and lacklustre because their blood glucose levels have fallen overnight. Food and liquid raise blood glucose and prevent dehydration. Get into the breakfast habit and zing into life—there are lots of options and no excuses for missing out!

Personal best every day

This is lifestyle eating and it has to be just right. Key features of the best everyday breakfasts are familiarity, personal favorites, and practicality—they have to be quick and easy. Single people, couples, busy parents, children, and teenagers have different takes on breakfast—weekends may bring room to maneuver but Monday to Friday has to be easy on the brain! Everyone needs to be fed and watered—some older children can help feed themselves but some adolescents need to be persuaded to eat (they *really* need to eat breakfast).

Food to keep going

The ideal combination is some fast-acting source of energy for a wide-awake buzz (a large glass of juice is great) backed up by slow-release foods that will provide fuel until the next meal. Most times, morning food is designed to get you going with minimum effort and maximum return—cereals, fruit, breakfast breads, muffins, toast, and yogurt are typical.

Carbohydrates are important, especially the type that break down slowly, releasing energy over a few hours. Those are the complex carbohydrates—starches rather than sugars. The glycaemic index is a scale that rates the

speed with which carbohydrates are broken down and absorbed compared to glucose. It gives values of 0–100 known as GI values. The higher the value, the quicker the food is absorbed (glucose has a value of 100). Eating slow-release foods (low GI value) helps to avoid hunger pangs and lack of energy.

High-fiber foods that are not highly processed (and not high sugar) provide energy for a few hours. Bran cereals and oatmeal are low GI and tortilla wraps, croissants, and whole wheat bread are medium GI. Apples, pears, grapefruit, oranges, grapes, berries, and bananas that are not too ripe are all low GI. Combining slow-release foods with others that provide instant energy slows down the energy rush. Fats and proteins slow down the process. Poached eggs, tomatoes, and mushrooms with toast, followed by fruit, is a good mix. Homemade muesli is excellent—oats, grains, nuts, dried fruit, with milk, provide a great mix of nutrients, with 'good' fat and protein from nuts, minerals and vitamins, especially if served with berries, apple or mango.

All days: all sorts

Breakfast is wonderfully versatile—savory or sweet, delicate or substantial, food can be eaten in formal style or on the move.

It's good to eat a variety of breakfasts—cereals some days; fruit bran muffins another; waffles with banana, nuts and yogurt; pancakes with eggs; toast with peanut butter followed by fruit; or yogurt with fruit, nuts, and seeds. When time is tight, a smoothie can be whizzed and drunk in seconds (or prepared ahead and chilled).

Time to indulge

On birthday weekends, bank holidays, when friends stay, for an anniversary or Christmas...indulgent breakfasts are superlative! Scrambled eggs with smoked salmon, a classic cooked breakfast, or what about sweet treats, such as pancakes or warm croissants with home-made jam?

1

Rise & Shine

serves 2

3 large ripe sweetie
grapefruit or ugli fruit

2/3 cup sparkling water

1 tbsp runny honey (optional)

some slices of lime or
peeled kiwi

2 tbsp yogurt

wake up sweetie

Halve the sweetie grapefruit or the ugli fruit and squeeze into
two glasses.

Add the water, and honey if liked.

Serve with a slice or two of lime or kiwi, floated on the surface
and top with a spoonful of yogurt.

serves 2

1 cup carrot juice

4 tomatoes, skinned,
seeded, and coarsely
chopped

1 tbsp lemon juice

scant 1/3 cup fresh parsley

1 tbsp grated fresh
gingerroot

6 ice cubes, crushed

1/2 cup water

chopped fresh parsley,
to garnish

carrot & ginger energizer

Put the carrot juice, tomatoes, and lemon juice into a food processor and process gently until combined.

Add the parsley to the food processor along with the ginger and ice cubes. Process until well combined, then pour in the water and process until smooth.

Pour the mixture into glasses and garnish with chopped fresh parsley. Serve at once.

serves 2

1 cup carrot juice

1 cup tomato juice

2 large red bell peppers,
seeded and coarsely chopped

1 tbsp lemon juice

freshly ground black pepper

carrot & red bell pepper booster

Pour the carrot juice and tomato juice into a food processor and process gently until combined.

Add the red bell peppers and lemon juice. Season with plenty of freshly ground black pepper and process until smooth.

Pour the mixture into tall glasses, then add straws and serve.

serves 2

2 large ripe Bartlett or
similar juicy pears

juice of 4 medium oranges

4 cubes candied ginger

pear, orange & ginger reviver

Peel the pears and cut into quarters, removing the cores. Put into
a food processor with the orange juice and the candied ginger
and process until smooth.

Pour into glasses and serve.

serves 2

1 wedge of watermelon,
weighing about 12 oz/350 g

ice cubes

1–2 fresh mint sprigs,
to garnish

watermelon refresher

Cut the rind off the watermelon. Chop the watermelon into chunks, discarding any seeds.

Put the watermelon chunks into a food processor and process until smooth.

Place ice cubes in two glasses. Pour the watermelon mixture over the ice and serve garnished with the mint.

serves 2–3

scant 1 cup whole blanched almonds

2¹/₂ cups milk

2 ripe bananas, halved

1 tsp natural vanilla extract

ground cinnamon, for sprinkling

almond & banana smoothie

Put the almonds into a food processor and process until very finely chopped.

Add the milk, bananas, and vanilla extract and blend until smooth and creamy. Pour into glasses and sprinkle with cinnamon.

serves 1

1 banana, sliced

1/2 cup fresh strawberries, hulled

2/3 cup plain yogurt

banana & strawberry smoothie

Put the banana, strawberries, and yogurt into a food processor and process for a few seconds until smooth.

Pour into a glass and serve at once.

serves 1

1/8 cup blueberries

3/8 cup raspberries,
thawed if frozen

1 tsp honey

scant 1 cup plain yogurt

about 1 heaped tbsp
crushed ice

1 tbsp sesame seeds

berry smoothie

Put the blueberries into a food processor and process for
1 minute.

Add the raspberries, honey, and yogurt and process for an
additional minute.

Add the ice and sesame seeds and process again for an
additional minute.

Pour into a tall glass and serve at once.

serves 2

1 cup orange juice

1/2 cup plain yogurt

2 eggs

2 bananas, sliced and frozen

slice of fresh banana,
to garnish

breakfast smoothie

Pour the orange juice and yogurt into a food processor and process gently until combined.

Add the eggs and frozen bananas and process until smooth.

Pour the mixture into glasses and garnish the rims with a slice of fresh banana.

serves 2

2 ripe bananas

2 tbsp sour cream

1/2 cup milk

2 tbsp clear honey,
plus extra for drizzling

1/2 tsp vanilla extract

banana breakfast shake

Put the bananas, sour cream, milk, honey, and vanilla extract into a food processor and process until smooth.

Pour into glasses and serve at once, drizzled with a little more honey on top.

Healthy Start

serves 4

¹/2 cup no-soak dried
peaches

¹/2 cup no-soak dried
apricots

¹/3 cup no-soak dried
pineapple chunks

2 oz/55 g no-soak dried
mango slices

1 cup unsweetened clear
apple juice

4 tbsp plain yogurt (optional)

exotic dried fruit compote

Put the dried fruit into a small pan with the apple juice. Bring slowly to a boil, then reduce the heat to low, cover, and let simmer for 10 minutes.

Spoon into serving dishes and top each serving with a tablespoon of yogurt, if desired. Serve at once.

serves 4

1 pink grapefruit

1 yellow grapefruit

3 oranges

citrus zing

Using a sharp knife, carefully cut away all the peel and pith from the grapefruit and oranges.

Working over a bowl to catch the juice, carefully cut the grapefruit and orange segments between the membranes to obtain skinless segments of fruit. Discard any seeds.

Add the segments to the bowl and gently mix together. Cover and let chill until required or divide among 4 serving dishes and serve at once.

serves 2

1 small charentais,
cantaloupe, or galia melon

2 kiwis

melon & kiwi fruit bowl

Cut the melon into quarters and remove and discard the seeds. Remove the melon flesh from the skin with a sharp knife and cut into chunks, or if you have a melon baller, scoop out as much of the melon flesh as possible and place in a bowl.

Peel the kiwis and cut the flesh into slices. Add to the melon and gently mix together. Cover and let chill until required or divide among 2 serving dishes and serve at once.

serves 4

3 tbsp honey

5/8 cup mixed unsalted nuts

8 tbsp plain yogurt

7/8 cup fresh blueberries

yogurt with honey, nuts & blueberries

Heat the honey in a small pan over medium heat. Add the nuts and stir until they are well coated. Remove from the heat and let cool slightly.

Divide the yogurt among 4 serving bowls, then spoon over the nut mixture and blueberries.

serves 2

1 cup jumbo oats

3/4 cup apple juice

1 red apple, cored

1 tbsp lemon juice

scant 1/4 cup chopped
toasted hazelnuts

1/2 tsp ground cinnamon

scant 1/2 cup plain yogurt

2 tbsp runny honey (optional)

21/2 oz/70 g fresh blueberries

blueberry muesli

Put the oats and apple juice in a bowl, then cover with plastic wrap and let soak in the refrigerator for an hour, or overnight. Grate or chop the apple and mix with the lemon juice to prevent discoloration.

Add the apple, hazelnuts, and cinnamon to the oat mixture and mix well.

Spoon the mixture into serving bowls and top with the yogurt. Drizzle over the honey, if using. Spoon the blueberries over the muesli and serve.

serves 4

for the granola

¼ oz/10 g rolled oats

⅛ oz/5 g sesame seeds

pinch of ground ginger

⅛ oz/5 g sunflower seeds

2 tsp freshly squeezed
orange juice

1 tsp runny honey

for the fruit cocktail

10½ oz/300 g seeded
watermelon, cut into chunks

3½ oz/100 g fresh orange
segments

6 tbsp freshly squeezed
orange juice

1 tsp finely grated
orange zest

1 tsp peeled and finely
sliced gingerroot

1 tsp runny honey

½ tsp arrowroot, blended
with a little cold water

watermelon, orange & ginger cocktail with granola

Preheat the oven to 350°F/180°C.

To make the granola, put all the dry ingredients into a bowl, then add the orange juice and honey and mix thoroughly. Spread out on a non-stick baking tray and bake for 7–8 minutes. Remove from the oven, break up into pieces, then return to the oven for a further 7–8 minutes. Remove from the oven and break up again. Leave to cool on the baking sheet. The mixture will become crunchy when cool.

To make the fruit cocktail, put the watermelon and orange segments into a bowl. Put the orange juice and zest, ginger and honey into a small saucepan over a medium heat and bring to the boil. Gradually stir in the arrowroot mixture and cook, stirring constantly, until thickened.

Pour the mixture over the fruit and leave to cool. Cover and chill in the fridge.

Spoon the fruit into glasses and sprinkle over the granola.

serves 4

12 large portobello mushrooms, wiped over and stems removed

2 tbsp corn oil, plus extra for oiling

1 fennel bulb, stalks removed, finely chopped

scant ½ cup sun-dried tomatoes, finely chopped

2 garlic cloves, crushed

1 cup grated fontina cheese

scant ½ cup freshly grated Parmesan cheese

3 tbsp chopped fresh basil

salt and pepper

1 tbsp olive oil

fresh Parmesan cheese shavings

1 tbsp chopped fresh parsley

stuffed portobello mushrooms with shaved parmesan

Preheat the oven to 350°F/180°C. Lightly oil a large ovenproof dish. Place 8 of the mushrooms, cup-side up, in the dish and chop the remaining 4 mushrooms finely.

Heat the corn oil in a nonstick skillet, add the chopped mushrooms, fennel, sun-dried tomatoes, and garlic and cook over low heat until the vegetables are soft but not browned. Remove from the heat and let cool.

When cool, add the grated cheeses, basil, and salt and pepper to taste. Mix well. Brush the mushrooms lightly with the olive oil and fill each cavity with a spoonful of the vegetable filling. Bake for 20–25 minutes, or until the mushrooms are tender and the filling is heated through.

Top with Parmesan shavings and parsley and serve at once, allowing 2 mushrooms for each person.

serves 4

10 1/2 oz/300 g asparagus, trimmed

1 tbsp white wine vinegar

4 large eggs

3 oz/85 g Parmesan cheese

pepper

asparagus with poached eggs & parmesan

Bring a pan of water to a boil. Add the asparagus to one pan, return to a simmer, and cook for 5 minutes, or until just tender.

Meanwhile, to poach the eggs, reduce the heat of the second skillet to a simmer and add the vinegar. When the water is barely simmering, carefully break the eggs into the skillet. Poach the eggs for 3 minutes, or until the whites are just set but the yolks are still soft.

Drain the asparagus and divide among 4 warmed plates. Top each plate of asparagus with an egg and shave over the cheese. Season to taste with pepper and serve at once.

serves 4

8 oz/225 g broccoli

1 tbsp white wine vinegar

4 eggs

8 oz/225 g smoked salmon

wholewheat bread, to serve

for the dressing

2/3 cup lowfat cream cheese

1–1¹/₂ tsp Dijon mustard

2 tsp snipped fresh chives

smoked salmon with broccoli & poached eggs

Divide the broccoli into spears, then cook in boiling water for 5–6 minutes, or until tender. Drain and keep warm while you poach the eggs.

To poach the eggs, fill a skillet three-quarters full with water and bring to a boil over low heat. Reduce the heat to a simmer and add the vinegar. When the water is barely simmering, carefully break the eggs into the skillet. Poach the eggs for 3 minutes, or until the whites are just set but the yolks are still soft.

Meanwhile, divide the smoked salmon among four individual plates. Stir all the dressing ingredients together in a mixing cup until blended.

Place the broccoli spears on the plates and top with a poached egg, then spoon over a little dressing and serve. Serve with wholewheat bread.

serves 4

1 tbsp olive oil

3 shallots, finely chopped

1 lb 2 oz/500 g baby spinach leaves

4 tbsp light cream

freshly grated nutmeg

pepper

4 large eggs

4 tbsp Parmesan cheese, finely grated

baked eggs with spinach

Preheat the oven to 400°F/200°C. Heat the oil in a skillet over medium heat, add the shallots, and cook, stirring frequently, for 4–5 minutes, or until soft. Add the spinach, cover, and cook for 2–3 minutes, or until the spinach has wilted. Remove the lid and cook until all the liquid has evaporated.

Add the cream to the spinach and season to taste with nutmeg and pepper. Spread the spinach mixture over the base of 4 shallow gratin dishes and make a well in the mixture with the back of a spoon.

Crack an egg into each well and sprinkle over the cheese. Bake in the preheated oven for 10–12 minutes, or until the eggs are set. Serve at once.

3

The
Big Breakfast

serves 4

1 tbsp white wine vinegar

4 eggs

4 English muffins

4 slices good-quality ham

for the quick hollandaise sauce

3 egg yolks

7 oz/200 g butter

1 tbsp lemon juice

pepper

eggs benedict with quick hollandaise sauce

To poach the eggs, fill a skillet three-quarters full with water and bring to a boil over low heat. Reduce the heat to a simmer and add the vinegar. When the water is barely simmering, carefully break the eggs into the skillet. Poach the eggs for 3 minutes, or until the whites are just set but the yolks are still soft.

Meanwhile, to make the hollandaise sauce, place the egg yolks in a food processor. Melt the butter in a small pan until bubbling. With the motor running, gradually add the hot butter to the food processor in a steady stream until the sauce is thick and creamy. Add the lemon juice, and a little warm water if the sauce is too thick, then season to taste with pepper. Remove from the food processor and keep warm.

Split the muffins and toast them on both sides. To serve, top each muffin with a slice of ham, a poached egg, and a generous spoonful of hollandaise sauce.

serves 2

10½ oz/300 g white mushrooms

1 tbsp butter

1 tbsp vegetable oil

salt and pepper

1 small fresh red chile, seeded and finely chopped

1 tbsp sour cream

2 tbsp chopped fresh parsley

1 tbsp chopped fresh rosemary

slices of ciabatta bread, toasted

extra-virgin olive oil

handful of arugula leaves

mushrooms with rosemary, chile, sour cream & arugula

Wipe the mushrooms with a damp cloth and slice thinly.

Heat the butter and vegetable oil in a wide sauté pan and add the mushrooms, stirring until well coated. Season lightly with salt and pepper and add the chopped chile. Cover and cook for 1–2 minutes, or until the mushrooms have softened, then stir in the sour cream. Sprinkle over the chopped parsley and rosemary.

Serve with slices of toasted ciabatta, drizzled lightly with olive oil and topped with a few arugula leaves.

serves 2

4 eggs

⅓ cup light cream

salt and pepper

2 tbsp snipped fresh chives, plus 4 whole fresh chives, to garnish

2 tbsp butter

4 slices brioche loaf, lightly toasted

chive scrambled eggs with brioche

Break the eggs into a medium bowl and whisk gently with the cream. Season to taste with salt and pepper and add the snipped chives.

Melt the butter in a non stick pan over medium heat, pour in the egg mixture, and cook, stirring gently with a wooden spoon, for 5–6 minutes, or until lightly set.

Place the toasted brioche slices in the center of 2 plates and spoon over the scrambled eggs. Serve at once, garnished with chives.

serves 6

2 oz/55 g butter, plus extra, melted, for greasing

⅓ cup all-purpose flour

⅔ cup milk

1 cup ricotta cheese

4 egg yolks

2 tbsp finely chopped fresh parsley

2 tbsp finely chopped fresh thyme

1 tbsp finely chopped fresh rosemary

salt and pepper

6 egg whites

scant 1 cup light cream

6 tbsp grated Parmesan cheese

sautéed white mushrooms, to serve

cheese & herb soufflés with sautéed mushrooms

Preheat the oven to 350°F/180°C. Brush six 3½-inch/9-cm soufflé dishes well with melted butter and set aside. Melt the butter in a medium pan, add the flour, and cook for 30 seconds, stirring constantly. Whisk in the milk and continue whisking over low heat until the mixture thickens. Cook for an additional 30 seconds. Remove from the heat and beat in the ricotta. Add the egg yolks and herbs and season well with salt and pepper.

Beat the egg whites in a clean bowl until they form stiff peaks then gently fold them through the ricotta mixture. Spoon into the prepared dishes, filling them just to the top. Place in a baking dish and pour in enough boiling water to come halfway up the sides of the dishes. Bake for 15–20 minutes, or until the soufflés are well risen and browned. Remove from the oven, let cool for 10 minutes, then gently ease out of their molds. Place in a lightly greased ovenproof dish and cover with plastic wrap.

Increase the oven temperature to 400°F/200°C. Remove the plastic wrap and pour the cream evenly over the soufflés, sprinkle with Parmesan, and return to the oven for an additional 15 minutes. Serve at once with sautéed mushrooms.

serves 4

8 eggs

⅓ cup light cream

2 tbsp chopped fresh dill,
plus extra for garnishing

salt and pepper

3½ oz/100 g smoked salmon,
cut into small pieces

2 tbsp butter

slices rustic bread, toasted

scrambled eggs with smoked salmon

Break the eggs into a large bowl and whisk together with the cream and dill. Season to taste with salt and pepper. Add the smoked salmon and mix to combine.

Melt the butter in a large nonstick skillet and pour in the egg and smoked salmon mixture. Using a wooden spatula, gently scrape the egg away from the sides of the skillet as it starts to set and swirl the skillet slightly to allow the uncooked egg to fill the surface.

When the eggs are almost cooked but still creamy, remove from the heat and spoon onto the prepared toast. Serve at once, garnished with a sprig of dill.

serves 6

5½ oz/150 g feta cheese, crumbled

1 cup ricotta cheese

5½ oz/150 g smoked salmon, diced

2 tbsp chopped fresh dill

2 tbsp snipped fresh chives

salt and pepper

12 sheets phyllo pastry

3½ oz/100 g butter, melted, plus extra for greasing

4 tbsp dried bread crumbs

6 tsp fennel seeds

smoked salmon, feta & dill phyllo packages

Preheat the oven to 350°F/180°C. Lightly grease a baking sheet. In a large bowl, combine the feta, ricotta, smoked salmon, dill, and chives. Season to taste.

Lay out a sheet of pastry on your counter and brush well with melted butter. Sprinkle over 2 teaspoons of the bread crumbs and cover with a second sheet of pastry. Brush with butter and spread a large tablespoon of the salmon mixture on one end of the pastry. Roll the pastry up, folding in the sides, to enclose the salmon completely and create a neat package. Place on the prepared baking sheet, brush the top of the package with butter and sprinkle over 1 teaspoon of the fennel seeds. Repeat with the remaining ingredients to make 6 packages.

Bake the packages for 25–30 minutes, or until the pastry is golden brown. Serve the packages warm.

serves 2–4

4 oz/115 g cooked shelled shrimp, thawed if frozen

4 scallions, chopped

2 oz/55 g zucchini, grated

4 eggs, separated

few dashes of Tabasco sauce, to taste

3 tbsp milk

salt and pepper

1 tbsp corn or olive oil

1 oz/25 g sharp Cheddar cheese, grated

fluffy shrimp omelet

Pat the shrimp dry with paper towels, then mix with the scallions and zucchini in a bowl and set aside.

Using a fork, beat the egg yolks with the Tabasco, milk, and salt and pepper to taste in a separate bowl.

Using an electric mixer or hand whisk, whisk the egg whites in a clean bowl until stiff peaks form. Gently stir the egg yolk mixture into the egg whites, taking care not to overmix.

Heat the oil in a large, nonstick skillet and when hot pour in the egg mixture. Cook over low heat for 4–6 minutes, or until lightly set. Meanwhile, preheat the broiler.

Spoon the shrimp mixture on top of the eggs and sprinkle with the cheese. Cook under the preheated broiler for 2–3 minutes, or until set and the top is golden brown. Cut into wedges and serve at once.

serves 6

butter, for greasing

1 lb 2 oz/500 g prepared basic
pie dough

all-purpose flour, for rolling

2 tbsp whole-grain mustard

12 lean bacon slices, diced,
cooked, and drained well

12 small eggs

pepper

1 cup grated Cheddar cheese

2 tbsp chopped fresh parsley

mini bacon & egg pastries with cheddar

Preheat the oven to 350°F/180°C. Lightly grease a deep 12-cup muffin pan.

Roll the dough out to a ¼ inch/5 mm thickness on a lightly floured counter and cut out 12 circles approximately 5 inches/ 13 cm in diameter. Use to line the cups of the muffin pan, gently pleating the sides of the dough as you ease it into the molds. Place ½ teaspoon of the mustard into the base of each pastry shell and top with a little of the bacon.

Break an egg into a cup, spoon the yolk into the pastry shell, then add enough of the white to fill the pastry shell about two-thirds full. Do not overfill. Season to taste with pepper and sprinkle the grated cheese evenly over the tops of the pastries. Bake for 20–25 minutes, or until the egg is set and the cheese is golden brown. Serve warm, sprinkled with chopped parsley.

serves 6

2 red bell peppers, halved and seeded

2 small chorizo sausages, diced

1 tbsp olive oil

2 potatoes, peeled and diced

handful of fresh basil leaves, torn into pieces

6 large eggs, lightly beaten

6 tbsp grated Manchego cheese

salt and pepper

tortilla with roasted bell peppers & spicy chorizo

Preheat the oven to 400°F/200°C. Place the red bell peppers on a lined baking sheet and roast for 15 minutes, or until the skins are black. Remove from the oven and cover with a dish cloth until cool. When cool, peel away the skins and dice the flesh.

Meanwhile, cook the diced chorizo in a 12-inch/30-cm nonstick skillet until it is brown and the fat is rendered. Drain on paper towels. Wipe out the skillet, then heat the oil and cook the diced potatoes for 5 minutes, or until soft and lightly browned. Return the chorizo to the skillet with the potatoes and add the diced red bell peppers and torn basil leaves.

Mix the eggs and grated cheese together and season to taste with salt and pepper. Pour over the ingredients in the skillet, using a wooden spoon to distribute the ingredients evenly. Let cook for a few minutes over low heat until the egg has started to set. To finish the tortilla, place the skillet under a preheated hot broiler to brown lightly. Slide onto a serving plate and cut into wedges to serve.

serves 4

8 lean Canadian bacon slices

2 beefsteak tomatoes or
4 tomatoes, halved

4 eggs

3 tbsp milk

salt and pepper

1 tbsp snipped fresh chives

1 tbsp unsalted butter

bacon & tomato with scrambled eggs

Preheat the broiler to high and cover the broiler rack with foil. Arrange the bacon on the foil and cook under the preheated broiler for 3–4 minutes on each side, or until crisp. About 3 minutes before the end of cooking time, add the tomatoes, cut-side up, and cook for the remainder of the cooking time.

Meanwhile, beat the eggs, milk, and salt and pepper to taste in a medium-size bowl, then stir in the chives.

Melt the butter in a nonstick pan over medium heat, pour in the egg mixture, and cook, stirring gently with a wooden spoon, for 5–6 minutes, or until lightly set.

Arrange the egg scramble with the cooked bacon and tomatoes on warmed serving plates and serve at once.

Sweet Treats

serves 6

175 g/6 oz all-purpose flour

2 tsp baking powder

½ tsp salt

2 tsp superfine sugar

2 eggs, separated

250 ml/9 fl oz milk

85 g/3 oz butter, melted

100 g/3½ oz butter,
cut into pieces

3 tbsp dark corn syrup

3 large ripe bananas, peeled
and thickly sliced

waffles with caramelized bananas

Mix the flour, baking powder, salt and sugar together in a bowl. Whisk the egg yolks, milk and melted butter together with a fork, then stir this mixture into the dry ingredients to make a smooth batter.

Using an electric mixer or hand whisk, whisk the egg whites in a clean bowl until stiff peaks form. Fold into the batter mixture. Spoon 2 large tablespoons of the batter into a preheated waffle maker and cook according to the manufacturer's instructions.

To make the caramelized bananas, melt the butter with the dark corn syrup in a saucepan over a low heat and stir until combined. Leave to simmer for a few minutes until the caramel thickens and darkens slightly. Add the bananas and mix gently to coat. Pour over the warm waffles and serve immediately.

serves 6

200 g/7 oz self-rising flour

100 g/3½ oz superfine sugar

1 tsp ground cinnamon

1 egg

200 ml/7 fl oz milk

2 apples, peeled and grated

1 tsp butter

for the maple syrup

85 g/3 oz butter, softened

3 tbsp maple syrup

apple crêpes with maple syrup butter

Mix the flour, sugar and cinnamon together in a bowl and make a well in the center. Beat the egg and the milk together and pour into the well. Using a wooden spoon, gently incorporate the dry ingredients into the liquid until well combined, then stir in the grated apple.

Heat the butter in a large non-stick skillet over low heat until melted and bubbling. Add tablespoons of the crêpes mixture to form 3½-inch/9-cm circles. Cook each crêpes for about 1 minute, until it starts to bubble lightly on the top and looks set, then flip it over and cook the other side for 30 seconds, or until cooked through. The crêpes should be golden brown; if not, increase the heat a little. Remove from the skillet and keep warm. Repeat the process until all of the crêpe batter has been used up (it is not necessary to add extra butter).

To make the maple syrup butter, melt the remaining butter with the maple syrup in a saucepan over low heat and stir until combined. To serve, place the crêpes on serving dishes and spoon over the flavored butter. Serve warm.

serves 5–6

1 cup all-purpose flour

2 tbsp superfine sugar

2 tsp baking powder

1/2 tsp salt

scant 1 cup buttermilk

3 tbsp unsalted butter, melted

1 large egg

5 oz/140 g fresh blueberries, plus extra to serve

sunflower-seed or corn oil, for oiling

butter

warm maple syrup, to serve

blueberry crêpes

Preheat the oven to 275°F/140°C. Sift the flour, sugar, baking powder, and salt together into a large bowl and make a well in the center.

Beat the buttermilk, butter, and egg together in a separate small bowl, then pour the mixture into the well in the dry ingredients. Beat the dry ingredients into the liquid, gradually drawing them in from the side, until a smooth batter is formed. Gently stir in the blueberries.

Heat a large skillet over medium-high heat until a splash of water dances on the surface. Using a pastry brush or crumpled piece of paper towel, oil the base of the skillet.

Drop about 4 tablespoons of batter separately into the skillet and spread each out into a 4-inch/10-cm circle. Continue adding as many crêpes as will fit in your skillet. Cook until small bubbles appear on the surface, then flip over with a spatula and cook the crêpes on the other side for an additional 1–2 minutes, or until the bases are golden brown.

Transfer the crêpes to a warmed plate and keep warm in the preheated oven while you cook the remaining batter, lightly oiling the skillet as before. Make a stack of the crêpes with parchment paper in between the crêpes.

Serve stacks of crêpes with a pat of butter on top and warmed maple syrup for pouring, garnished with blueberries.

serves 4–5

2/3 cup all-purpose flour

scant 1/4 cup unsweetened cocoa

pinch of salt

1 egg

2 tbsp superfine sugar

11/2 cups milk

scant 2 tbsp unsalted butter

confectioners' sugar, for dusting

ice cream or pouring cream, to serve

for the berry compote

51/2 oz/150 g fresh blackberries

51/2 oz/150 g fresh blueberries

8 oz/225 g fresh raspberries

1/4 cup superfine sugar

juice of 1/2 lemon

1/2 tsp allspice (optional)

chocolate crêpes with berry compote

Preheat the oven to 275°F/140°C. Sift the flour, unsweetened cocoa, and salt together into a large bowl and make a well in the center.

Beat the egg, sugar, and half the milk together in a separate bowl, then pour the mixture into the dry ingredients. Beat the dry ingredients into the liquid, gradually drawing them in from the side, until a batter is formed. Gradually beat in the remaining milk. Pour the batter into a pitcher.

Heat a 7-inch/18-cm nonstick skillet over medium heat and add 1 teaspoon of the butter.

When the butter has melted, pour in enough batter just to cover the bottom, then swirl it round the skillet while tilting it so that you have a thin, even layer. Cook for 30 seconds and then lift up the edge of the crêpe to check if it is cooked. Loosen the crêpe around the edge, then flip it over with a spatula or palette knife. Alternatively, toss the crêpe by flipping the skillet quickly with a flick of the wrist and catching it carefully. Cook on the other side until the bottom is golden brown.

Transfer the crêpe to a warmed plate and keep warm in the preheated oven while you cook the remaining batter, adding the remaining butter to the skillet as necessary. Make a stack of the crêpes with parchment paper in between the crêpes.

To make the compote, pick over the berries and put in a pan with the sugar, lemon juice, and allspice, if using. Cook over low heat until the sugar has dissolved and the berries are warmed through. Do not overcook.

Put a crêpe on a warmed serving plate and spoon some of the compote onto the center. Either roll or fold the crêpe and dust with confectioners' sugar. Repeat with the remaining crêpes. Serve with ice cream or pouring cream.

serves 4

4 eggs, plus 1 extra egg white

1/4 tsp ground cinnamon

1/4 tsp allspice

scant 1/2 cup superfine sugar

1/4 cup freshly squeezed orange juice

101/2 oz/300 g mixed fresh seasonal berries, such as strawberries, raspberries, and blueberries, picked over and hulled

4 slices thick white bread

1 tbsp unsalted butter, melted

fresh mint sprigs, to decorate

spiced french toast with seasonal berries

Preheat the oven to 425°F/220°C. Put the eggs and egg white in a large, shallow bowl or dish and whisk together with a fork. Add the cinnamon and allspice and whisk until combined.

To prepare the berries, put the sugar and orange juice in a pan and bring to a boil over low heat, stirring until the sugar has dissolved. Add the berries, then remove from the heat and let cool for 10 minutes.

Meanwhile, soak the bread slices in the egg mixture for about 1 minute on each side. Brush a large baking sheet with the melted butter and place the bread slices on the sheet. Bake in the preheated oven for 5–7 minutes, or until lightly browned. Turn the slices over and bake for an additional 2–3 minutes. Serve the berries spooned over the toast and decorated with mint sprigs.

serves 8

1¹/8 sticks butter, softened,
plus extra for greasing

¹/2 cup superfine sugar

¹/4 cup soft brown sugar

3 eggs

1 tsp vanilla extract

3 large, ripe bananas

1²/3 cups self-rising flour

1 tsp freshly grated nutmeg

1 tsp ground cinnamon

mascarpone cheese or plain
yogurt, to serve

confectioners' sugar, sifted,
for dusting (optional)

for the strawberry compote

scant ¹/2 cup soft brown
sugar

juice of 2 oranges

grated rind of 1 orange

1 cinnamon stick

14 oz/400 g fresh
strawberries, hulled
and thickly sliced

banana bread with strawberry compote & mascarpone

Preheat the oven to 350ºF/180ºC. Grease a 9 x 4¹/4-inch/23 x 11-cm loaf pan and line the base with nonstick parchment paper.

Put the butter and sugars in a bowl and beat together until light and fluffy. Mix in the eggs, one at a time, then mix in the vanilla extract. Peel the bananas and mash roughly with a fork. Stir gently into the batter mixture, then add the flour, nutmeg, and cinnamon, stirring until just combined.

Pour the mixture into the prepared pan and bake in the preheated oven for 1¹/4 hours, or until a skewer inserted into the center comes out clean. Let stand in the pan for 5 minutes before turning out onto a wire rack to cool.

To make the compote, put the sugar, orange juice and rind, and cinnamon stick in a pan and bring to a boil. Add the strawberries and return to a boil. Remove from the heat, then pour into a clean heatproof bowl and let cool. Remove the cinnamon stick. Serve slices of the banana bread with a dollop of mascarpone cheese or yogurt and spoon over the warm or cold compote. Dust with sifted confectioners' sugar if desired.

serves 4–8

scant 2½ cups self-rising
flour

pinch of salt

2 tbsp superfine sugar

1 tsp ground cinnamon

3½ oz/100 g butter, melted,
plus extra for greasing

2 egg yolks

scant 1 cup milk, plus extra
for glazing

for the filling

1 tsp ground cinnamon

¼ cup brown sugar

2 tbsp superfine sugar

1 tbsp butter, melted

for the frosting

1 cup confectioners' sugar,
sifted

2 tbsp cream cheese,
softened

1 tbsp butter, softened

about 2 tbsp boiling water

1 tsp vanilla extract

simple cinnamon rolls

Preheat the oven to 350°F/180°C. Grease an 8-inch/20-cm round pan and line the bottom with parchment paper.

Mix the flour, salt, superfine sugar, and cinnamon together in a bowl. Whisk the butter, egg yolks, and milk together and combine with the dry ingredients to make a soft dough. Turn out onto a large piece of waxed paper lightly sprinkled with flour, and roll out to a rectangle 12 x 10 inch/30 x 25 cm.

To make the filling, mix the ingredients together, spread evenly over the dough and roll up to form a log. Using a sharp knife, cut the dough into 8 even-size slices and pack into the prepared pan. Brush gently with extra milk and bake for 30–35 minutes, or until golden brown. Remove from the oven and let cool for 5 minutes before removing from the pan.

Sift the confectioners' sugar into a large bowl and make a well in the center. Place the cream cheese and butter in the center, pour over the water, and stir to mix. Add extra boiling water, a few drops at a time, until the frosting coats the back of a spoon. Stir in the vanilla extract. Drizzle over the rolls. Serve warm or cold.

serves 6–12

1 lb 2 oz/500 g white bread flour, plus extra for rolling

scant ¼ cup superfine sugar

1 tsp salt

2 tsp active dry yeast

1¼ cups milk, heated until just warm to the touch

10½ oz/300 g butter, softened, plus extra for greasing

1 egg, lightly beaten with 1 tbsp milk, for glazing

fresh croissants

Preheat the oven to 400°F/200°C. Stir the dry ingredients into a large bowl, make a well in the center, and add the milk. Mix to a soft dough, adding more milk if too dry. Knead on a lightly floured counter for 5–10 minutes, or until smooth and elastic. Let rise in a large greased bowl, covered, in a warm place until doubled in size. Meanwhile, flatten the butter with a rolling pin between 2 sheets of wax paper to form a rectangle about ¼ inch/5 mm thick, then let chill.

Knead the dough for 1 minute. Remove the butter from the refrigerator and let soften slightly. Roll out the dough on a well floured counter to 18 x 6 inch/46 x 15 cm. Place the butter in the center, folding up the sides and squeezing the edges together gently. With the short end of the dough toward you, fold the top third down toward the center, then fold the bottom third up. Rotate 90° clockwise so that the fold is to your left and the top flap toward your right. Roll out to a rectangle and fold again. If the butter feels soft, wrap the dough in plastic wrap, and let chill. Repeat the rolling process twice more. Cut the dough in half. Roll out one half into a triangle ¼ inch/5 mm thick (keep the other half refrigerated). Use a cardboard triangular template, base 7 inch/18 cm and sides 8 inch/20 cm, to cut out the croissants.

Brush the triangles lightly with the glaze. Roll into croissant shapes, starting at the base and tucking the point underneath to prevent unrolling while cooking. Brush again with the glaze. Place on an ungreased baking sheet and let double in size. Bake for 15–20 minutes until golden brown.

makes 5 x 1-lb/450-g jars

3 lb 8 oz/1.6 kg fresh
strawberries

3 tbsp lemon juice

3 lb/1.3 kg granulated or
preserving sugar

strawberry jam

Preheat the oven to 350°F/180°C. Sterilize five 1-lb/450-g jelly jars
with screw-top lids.

Pick over the strawberries and hull—discarding any that are
overripe. Put the fruit in a large pan with the lemon juice and heat
over low heat until some of the fruit juices begin to run. Continue
to simmer gently for 10–15 minutes, or until softened.

Add the sugar and stir until it has dissolved. Increase the heat and
boil rapidly for 2–3 minutes, or until setting point is reached. Test
the mixture with a sugar thermometer—it should read 221°F/
105°C for a good setting point. Alternatively, drop a teaspoonful of
jelly onto a cold saucer and place it in the refrigerator to cool it,
and then push it with your finger. If it forms a wrinkled skin, it is
ready. If not, boil for an additional minute and repeat.

Remove the pan from the heat and let cool for 15–20 minutes, to
prevent the fruit rising in the jar. Skim if necessary. Meanwhile,
warm the jars in the preheated oven. Remove and fill carefully
with the jelly, using a ladle and a jelly funnel. Top with wax disks,
waxed side down, and screw on the lids tightly. Wipe the jars clean
and let cool. Label and date to avoid confusion later.

Store in a cool, dry place. Once opened, it is advisable to keep the
jar in the refrigerator.

serves 5–10

2 cups self-rising wholewheat flour

2 tsp baking powder

2 tbsp brown sugar

$1/2$ cup no-soak dried apricots, finely chopped

1 banana, mashed with 1 tbsp orange juice

1 tsp finely grated orange rind

$1^{1}/4$ cups skim milk

1 large egg, beaten

3 tbsp sunflower-seed or peanut oil

2 tbsp rolled oats

fruit spread, honey, or maple syrup, to serve

fruit muffins

Preheat the oven to 400°F/200°C. Line 10 cups of a 12-cup muffin pan with muffin paper liners. Sift the flour and baking powder into a mixing bowl, adding any husks that remain in the strainer. Stir in the sugar and chopped apricots.

Make a well in the center and add the mashed banana, orange rind, milk, beaten egg, and oil. Mix together well to form a thick batter and divide evenly among the muffin liners.

Sprinkle with a few rolled oats and bake in the oven for 25–30 minutes until well risen and firm to the touch, or until a toothpick inserted into the center comes out clean.

Remove the muffins from the oven and place them on a cooling rack to cool slightly. Serve the muffins while still warm with a little fruit spread, honey, or maple syrup.